UNDER THE SEA
CROCHET

ADORABLE SEA CREATURES AMIGURUMI YOU'LL LOVE

Contents

FISH AMIGURUMI

MATERIALS

Worsted weight yarn. The colorways pictured in this pattern are Blue Mint, Grape, and Super Duper Yellow. You can also find this yarn here on Yarnspirations.

Safety eyes. If you'd like the option of crocheting the eyes rather than using safety eyes, here's a great tutorial!

Crochet hook. If you prefer to use a different size for amigurumi projects, feel free to use it! You just might end up with a slightly larger or smaller fish.

Stuffing - any fiber based stuffing to to stuff your amigurumi

Yarn needle - bent yarn needles work great for sewing pieces together!

STITCHES USED:

Ch - chain
Sl St - slip stitch
SC - single crochet

DC - double crochet

INV DEC - invisible single crochet decrease - insert hook into front loop of next stitch, then insert your hook into the front loop of the following stitch (3 loops on hook). Yarn over and draw through 2 loops (2 loops on hook), yarn over and pull through 2 remaining loops on hook.

IMPORTANT NOTES:

Magic Circle - Make a circle with your yarn, insert crochet hook into circle and draw up a loop. Use this loop to start your first chain 1 of the pattern.

Continuous Rounds - The head/body of the fish is worked in continuous rounds without joining. After you finish the stitches of one round, start right on the next without joining between. I find it handy to use a stitch marker (or a piece of yarn) to mark the start of each round so you know when each round starts/ends.

Color Changes - change colors at the end of the round in the last stitch of the round. Complete last single crochet of the round until the last yarn over. Yarn over with new color and pull through last step of the single crochet. So your single crochet will go like this: insert hook into last stitch, pull up a loop, yarn over with new color, pull through both loops on hook. Optional - To make your color changes even less noticeable, make your first stitch of the next round a slip stitch instead of a single crochet.

Stuff as you go - Add stuffing fish's head/body as you work it up. Make sure you are finished stuffing the body section before your decreases make the opening too narrow.

Finished Size - This fish amigurumi measures approximately 4.5" in length from tip of the nose to the end of the tail fin.

PATTERN

Body/Head

*Stuff the body as you go. Make sure you have added enough stuffing to the body before the opening gets too small while working the decrease rounds.

For the body, I used blue as the main color and then purple and yellow as the two accent colors. In this pattern, I'll call them main color (blue), accent color 1 (yellow) and accent color 2 (purple).

Round 1: In main color, magic circle, chain 1, 6 SC into ring. (6)

Round 2: SC in each stitch around (6)

Round 3: 2 SC in each stitch around (12)

Round 4: SC in each stitch around (12)

Round 5: 2 SC in first stitch, SC in next stitch, repeat around. (18)

Round 6: SC in each stitch around (18)

Round 7: 2 SC in first stitch, SC in next 2 stitches, repeat around (24)

Round 8: SC in each stitch around (24)

Round 9: 2 SC in first stitch, SC in next 3 stitches, repeat around (30)

Round 10: SC in each stitch around (30)

Change to accent color #1

Round 11: SC in each stitch around (30)

Change to main color

Rounds 12-13: SC in each stitch around (30)

Change to accent color #2

*Inserting safety eyes - Hold the fish so that the front is facing you and the seam where you can see your color changes is on the bottom of the fish's belly. Insert the safety eyes, one on each side of the fish, between rounds 6 and 7. Eyes will be approximately 5 stitches apart, if you count around the top of the head (or about 11 stitches apart (if you count around the bottom of the fish). Make sure that when you hold your fish facing you, that the eyes are lined up on either side of the head and directly opposite each other.

Round 14: SC in each stitch around (30)

5

Change to main color

Rounds 15-16: SC in each stitch around (30)

Change to accent color #1

Round 17: SC in each stitch around (30)

Change to main color

Rounds 18-19: SC in each stitch around (30)

Change to accent color #2

*Start stuffing the fish's body, if you haven't already. Continue stuffing as you work the next rounds, making sure that enough stuffing has been added before the opening is too small when working the decrease rounds.

Round 20: SC in each stitch around (30)

Change to main color

Round 21: SC in each stitch around (30)

Round 22: INV DEC, SC in next 3 stitches, repeat around (24)

Round 23: INV DEC, SC in next 2 stitches, repeat around (18)

Round 24: INV DEC, SC in next stitch, repeat around (12)

Round 25: INV DEC, repeat around (6)

Fasten off, weave in ends.

7

Tail Fin

Row 1: In main color, magic circle, ch 2, 4 DC into ring, change to accent color #1. Ch 2, turn. (4)

Row 2: 2 DC in each stitch, change to accent color #2. Ch 2, turn. (8)

Row 3: 3 DC into first stitch, slip stitch in next stitch, *3 DC in next stitch, slip stitch in next. Repeat from * across. (12 DC).

Fasten off. Weave in ends, leave the main color tail long enough to sew the tail to the body.

Side Fins (make 2)

Row 1: In accent color #1, magic circle, ch 2, 3 DC into ring, change to accent color #2. Ch 1, turn. (3)

Row 2: 2 SC in each stitch. (6)

Fasten off. Weave in ends. Leave one tail long to sew the fins on the body.

8

ATTACHING THE FINS TO THE BODY

Sew the tail fin to the back of the body. Be sure to hold the fish upright so that your tail is lined up vertically on the back of the body, and not sewn on sideways. You'll only be sewing around the bottom part of the fin that touches the fish (in the main color). Weave in ends and cut yarn.

Sew the fins to the sides of the body. Attach them at approximately round 16, right in front of the second band of accent color #1 (second band of yellow pictured below). Just sew around the first round of the fin that touches the fish and let the end of the fin stick out towards the sides.

That's it! Now you are all finished making your fish amigurumi!

9

BABY SHARK

MATERIALS

Yarn (light blue and white, I used 100% cotton, 90 m/25 g).
Crochet hook (I used 1,5 mm hook).
Plastic eyes size 4 mm, glue.
Sewing needle and scissors.
Fiberfill.
Size of the shark is about 8 cm.

ABBREVIATIONS

MR - magic (amigurumi) ring
ch - chain
sc - single crochet
hdc - half double crochet
inc - increase
dec - decrease
slst - slip stitch
w- white
b- blue

After preparing the materials, let's start making our amigurumi pattern.

PATTERN
Body
Start with blue.

Rnd 1. 6 sc in MR
Rnd 2. (1 sc, inc)*3 (9)
Rnd 3. (2 sc, inc)*3 (12)
Now add white yarn (w), do not cut the blue yarn (b).
Rnd 4. w - 3 sc, b - inc, 3 sc, inc, 3 sc, 1 sc, w - 1 sc into the same st. (15)
Rnd 5. w - 4 sc, b - inc, 4 sc, inc, 4 sc, 1 sc, w - 1 sc into the same st. (18)
Rnd 6. w - 5 sc, inc, b - 5 sc, inc, 5 sc, 1 sc, w - 1 sc into the same st. (21)
Rnd 7. w - 6 sc, inc, 1 sc, - b - 5 sc, inc, 6 sc, inc (24)
Rnd 8. w - 7 sc, inc, 2 sc, b - 5 sc, inc, 7 sc, inc (27)
Rnd 9. w - 11 sc, b - 16 sc (27)
Rnd 10. w - 8 sc, inc, 2 sc, b - 6 sc, inc, 8 sc, inc (30)
Rnd 11. w - 12 sc, b - 18 sc (30)
Rnd 12. w - 2 sc, inc, 9 sc, b - inc, 9 sc, inc, 7 sc (33)
Rnd 13. w - 13 sc, b - 20 sc (33)
Rnd 14. w - 13 sc, b - 20 sc (33)
Rnd 15. w - 6 sc, dec, 5 sc, b - 7 sc, dec, 9 sc, dec (30)
Rnd 16. w - 12 sc, b - 18 sc (30)

Rnd 17. w - 5 sc, dec, 5 sc, b - 6 sc, dec, 4 sc, dec, 4 sc (27)
Rnd 18. w - 11 sc, b - 16 sc (27)
Rnd 19. w - 4 sc, dec, 5 sc, b - 5 sc, dec, 4 sc, dec, 3 sc (24)
Rnd 20. w - 10 sc, b - 14 sc (24)
Start stuffing.
Rnd 21. w - 4 sc, dec, 4 sc, b - 4 sc, dec, 3 sc, dec, 3 sc (21)
Rnd 22. w - 9 sc, b- 12 sc (21)
Rnd 23. w - 3 sc, dec, 4 sc, b - 3 sc, dec, 3 sc, dec, 2 sc (18)
Rnd 24. w - 8 sc, b - 10 sc (18)
Rnd 25. w - 3 sc, dec, 3 sc, b - 2 sc, dec, 2 sc, dec, 2 sc (15)
Rnd 26. w - 7 sc, b - 8 sc (15)
Rnd 27. w - 3 sc, dec, 2 sc, b - 1 sc, dec, 2 sc, dec, 1 sc (12)
Rnd 28. w - 2 sc, dec, 2 sc, b - dec, 2 sc, dec (9)
Stuff to the end.
Cut the white yarn, secure it and weave in the ends. Cut the blue yarn and sew the opening with it, secure the thread, weave in the ends.

Side fins (make 2)
Blue yarn.
Rnd 1. 4 sc in MR
Rnd 2. (1 sc, inc)*2 (6)
Rnd 3. (1 sc, inc)*3 (9)
Rnd 4. 8 sc, inc (10)
Rnd 5-6. 10 sc (2 rounds)
Do not stuff. Leave a thread for sewing. Fold the edges together and sew them.

Tail fins (make 2)
Blue yarn.
Rnd 1. 4 sc in MR
Rnd 2. (1 sc, inc)*2 (6)
Rnd 3. (1 sc, inc)*3 (9)
Rnd 4. (1 sc, inc)*2, 5 sc (11)
Rnd 5. 11 sc
Rnd 6. 6 sc, dec, 3 sc (10)
Rnd 7. 5 sc (uncomplete round)
Do not stuff. Leave a thread for sewing.

Upper fin
Blue yarn.

Rnd 1. 4 sc in MR
Rnd 2. (1 sc, inc)*2 (6)
Rnd 3. (1 sc, inc)*3 (9)
Rnd 4. (2 sc, inc)*3 (12)
Rnd 5. 12 sc
Rnd 6. 4 sc, 4 hdc, 4 sc (12)
Do not stuff. Leave a thread for sewing.

Assembly
1. Sew tail fins on the back.
2. Sew on the side fins on rounds 16-19 around the color change line.
3. Sew on the upper fin on rounds 16-21.
4. Glue the eyes between 10th and 11th rounds on the sides, position them so that they are symmetrical according to the fins and the white part of the body.
5. Embroider a smile on 10th round.
6. Embroider 3 stripes on each side in front of the side fins.

Congratulations, you have completed the Baby Shark amigurumi pattern

14

OCTOPUS

MATERIALS

Main Color size 4 worsted weight yarn
Alternate Color size 4 worsted weight yarn
size 4 (G) hook
Yarn Needle
Polyfil
Rattle Noise Maker

ABBREVIATIONS

SC: single crochet
HDC: half double crochet
DC: double crochet
TRC: triple crochet
INC: two single crochet in one stitch
DEC:
Invisible decrease (Put hook through the FRONT LOOP ONLY of the two
stitches you are bringing together. Pull yarn through. You will have two loops on hook. Pull yarn through both loops)

PATTERN

Eyes:
6 DC in a magic circle. With white scrap yarn, sew on cute eye reflections. Make 2.
Have scrap black yarn for the smile ready to go.

For the head:
Round
1: In a magic circle, SC 6. Pull tight and add stitch marker. (For the rest of the pattern keep moving the stitch marker up to the last stitch)
Round 2: INC in each stitch around. (12)
Round 3: *SC in first stitch, INC in next* Repeat * * around. (18)
Round 4: *SC in first 2 stitches, INC in next* Repeat * * around. (24)
Round 5: *SC in first 3 stitches, INC in next.* Repeat * * around. (30)
Round 6: *SC in first 4 stitches, INC in next.* Repeat * * around. (36)
Round 7: *SC in first 5 stitches, INC

in next.* Repeat * * around. (42)

Round 8: *SC in first 6 stitches, INC in next.* Repeat * * around. (48)

Round 9: *SC in first 7 stitches, INC in next.* Repeat * * around. (54)

Round 10: *SC in first 8 stitches, INC in next.* Repeat * * around. (60)

Round 11-18: SC in each stitch around. (60)

(Sew on the eyes and mouth here)

Round 19: *SC in first 8 stitches, DEC in next.* Repeat * * around. (54)

Round 20: *SC in first 7 stitches, DEC in next.* Repeat * * around. (48)

Round 21: *SC in first 6 stitches, DEC in next.* Repeat * * around. (42)

Round 22: *SC in first 5 stitches, DEC in next.* Repeat * * around. (36)

(Start to stuff and add the rattle)

Round 23: *SC in first 4 stitches, DEC in next.* Repeat * * around. (30)

Round 24: *SC in first 3 stitches, DEC in next.* Repeat * * around. (24)

Round 25: *SC in first 2 stitches, DEC in next.* Repeat * * around. (18) (Finish stuffing)

Round 26: *SC in first stitch, DEC in next.* Repeat * * around. (12)

Round 27: DEC in each stitch around. Cut the yarn, leaving a long tail. Using the needle, sew the remaining gap closed. (6)

Tentacles:

With the accent color chain 30 and turn. SC in second chain from hook. HDC, HDC, DC, DC. TRC in the remaining chains. Cut yarn and sew in ends. Repeat with the main color, but DO NOT CUT YARN! Line up the two pieces. SC around the entire piece, with 2 SC where ever you need to turn.

Leave a long tail to sew on to the head.
Repeat 8 times.
Sew onto the head.

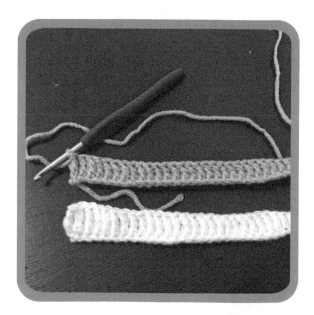

BLUE LOBSTER

18

MATERIALS

6mm hook;
Bernat Blanket yarn in two shades
of blue
Any light blue for main (less than
100g)
Any dark blue for accent (less than
50g)
However, you can use any size
6/Super Bulky yarn of choice or,
alternatively, here are some other
great options in Bernat Blanket:
Teal/Dark Teal, Blue Velvet/Lapis,
Ocean Teal Ombre (separating the
colours), Stripes Teal Deal
(separating the colours).
14mm Safety Eyes;
Stitch markers;
Stuffing;
Tapestry needle.

TERMS AND STITCHES:

Ch - Chain

MR - Magic Ring

Slst - Slip stitch

Sc - Single Crochet

Inc - Increase. Work a regular sc
increase

Invdec - Invisible decrees

FLO - Front loops only

BLO - Back loops only

Beg - Beginning

PATTERN
Body:

The body is worked from the bottom
up starting with the tail. The tail is
worked around a starting chain. The
pattern is worked in continuous
rounds.
Rnd 1: Ch 8, starting in 2nd ch from
hook, sc in each of the next 6 chs,
4sc into last ch, continue on
opposite side of chs, sc 4, 4sc into

last ch (18 sts)
Rnd 2: Sc in each st around (18 sts)
Rnd 3: *Sc 4, invdec, repeat from *
twice more (15 sts)
Rnd 4: *Sc 3, invdec, repeat from *
twice more (12 sts)
Rnd 5: Sc in each st (12 sts)
Stuff the tail.
Rnd 6: *Sc 3, inc, repeat from * twice
more (15 sts)
Rnd 7: *Sc 4, inc, repeat from * twice
more (18 sts)

Rnd 8: *Sc 2, inc, repeat from * five
more times (24 sts)

Rnd 8(a): Drop your working yarn
but do not tie off (pull up a long
loop or add a stitch marker to the
live loop so you don't lose it). Insert
your hook into the front loop of the
next st. Insert a stitch marker into
the back loop of the same st. Join
your dark blue yarn and work the
following: Slst into FLO of each st
(24 sts), slst to beg st, tie off.

Insert your hook into the live loop of
your main yarn in Row 8.

Rnd 9: Working in the BLO of Rnd 8
(i.e. where you placed your stitch
marker) *sc 5, inc, repeat from *
three more times (28 sts)

Rnd 10: Sc in each st (28 sts)

Rnd 10(a): Repeat row 8(a)

Rnd 11: Working in BLO of Rnd 10,
sc in each st (28 sts)

Rnd 12: Sc in each st (28 sts)

Rnd 12(a): Repeat row 8(a)

Rnd 13: Working in BLO of Rnd 12,
sc in each st (28 sts)

Rnd 14: Sc in each st (28 sts)

Rnd 15:*Sc 5, invdec, repeat from *
three more times (24 sts)

Rnd 16: *Sc 2, invdec, repeat from * five more times (18 sts)

Stuff the body. Insert 14mm safety eyes between rows 13 and 14 with approximately 4 sts between them. Stitch cheeks on if you wish.

Rnd 17: *Sc 1, invdec, repeat from * five more times (12 sts)

Rnd 18: Invdec 6 times (6 sts).

Top up stuffing. Tie off, leaving a long tail for closing. Weave yarn tail through each stitch and pull to close. Weave ends inside.

Antenna (make 2):
Row 1: In dark blue yarn, ch 8, starting in 2nd ch from hook, slst into the back bump of each ch (7 sts).

Tie off, leaving a tail for sewing.

Stitch onto the top of the head between rows 16 and 17 with approximately 5 sts between them. Weave in ends.

Claws (make 2):
Rnd 1: In light blue yarn, work 6 sc into MR (6 sts)

Rnd 2: *Sc, inc, repeat from * twice more (9 sts)

Rnd 3: *Sc 2, inc, repeat from * twice more (12 sts)

Rnd 4: *Sc 3, inc, repeat from * twice more (15 sts)

Rnd 5: Inc in first st, sc in each st around (16 sts)

Rnd 6: Invdec 8 times (8 sts)

Stuff the claw.

Rnd 7: *Sc 2, invdec, repeat from * once more (6 sts)

Rnds 8-10: Sc in each st (6 sts)

Tie off. If you would like the claws to be posable, insert pipe cleaners (chenille wire). Stitch claws onto each side of the body between the second and third dark blue stripe.

Legs (Make 4):
Row 1: Using dark blue yarn, ch 4, starting in 2nd ch from hook, slst into the back bump of each ch (3 sts).

Tie off. Stitch two legs onto each side of the body underneath each claw.

You're done!

CELIA THE CRAB

MATERIALS
Worsted Weight Yarn
Knit Picks Shine Worsted in Serrano
(~62 yards)
Color Of Choice For Bow (small
amount)
E/4 (3.50mm) crochet hook
Polyfil or stuffing of your choice
Yarn/Darning needle
Two 12mm plastic safety eyes
Black Embroidery floss (bell)
Embroidery needle (bell)
Scissors
Locking Stitch Markers (optional)

TECHNIQUES
Magic Circle
Single Crochet
Single Crochet Increase
Single Crochet Decrease (I like to
use an invisible decrease)
Slipknot
Chain
Slip Stitch
Fastening Off

Attaching Parts
Seamless Join

ABBREVIATIONS
sc - single crochet
st/sts - stitch(es)
inc - increase (add 2 stitches into a
stitch)
dec - decrease (join 2 stitches into
1)
ch - chain
sl st - slip stitch
R1- round 1
( ) - repeat this group of stitches

PATTERN EXAMPLE

6 sc into a Magic Circle {6 sts}
R1 starts with 6 single crochet in a
magic circle
Alternate way to begin: chain 2, sc 6
times in 2nd chain from hook {6
sts}

(inc, sc) 6 times {18 sts}
(2 single crochets into a stitch, then

single crochet in the next stitch) -
repeat that sequence a total of 6
times for a total of 18 stitches

(dec, sc in next 2 sts) 6 times {18 sts}
(join 2 single crochets into 1, and
then single crochet in next 2
stitches) - repeat that sequence a
total of 6 times for a total of 18
stitches

(sc, 3sc) 2 times {8 sts}
(single crochet in one stitch, then
three single crochet into the next
stitch) - repeat that sequence a
total of 2 times for a total of 8
stitches

HEAD AND BODY

R1: 4 sc into a magic circle {4 sts}
Alternate way to begin: chain 2, sc 4
times in 2nd chain from hook {4 sts}

R2: (sc, 3sc) 2 times {8 sts}

R3: (sc, 3sc) 4 times {16 sts}
R4: sc in next 2 sts, (3sc, sc in next 3 sts) 3 times, 3sc, sc in last st {24 sts}

R5: sc in next 3 sts, (3sc, sc in next 5 sts) 3 times, 3sc, sc in next 2 sts {32 sts}

R6: sc in next 4 sts, (3sc, sc in next 7 sts) 3 times, 3sc, sc in next 3 sts {40 sts}

R7: sc in back loop only in next 40 sts {40 sts}
Back to crocheting in both loops.

Back loop only

R8-15: sc in next 40 sts {40 sts}
R16: (dec, sc in next 3 sts) 8 times
{32 sts}
Embroider the eyes.

R1-R16. Begin by placing a pin in the middle of the piece, between R12/13. Thread a long piece of embroidery floss into an embroidery needle and knot one end. On the inside of the head, pick up a bit of yarn with your needle and make a knot.

Begin to embroider into the 2nd stitch to the right/left of the pin.

Insert your needle one round up and one stitch over between R11/12.

28

Go up through a stitch on R12/13 (leaving one stitch open between eyes) and back down through the stitch on R11/12.

Go back up through a corner stitch of the eye to start the eyelashes.

Insert your needle one round up to make the first eyelash.

Go back up through the corner of the eye and move your needle up to make the second eyelash. Secure with a knot on the inside of the head.

Repeat on the other side. Begin to embroider into the 2nd stitch to the right/left of the pin.

Begin to make the smile by going into the stitch next to the eye on R12/13. And then moving down and over one stitch on R13/14.

Go up through R12/13, leaving one stitch open between the smile.

Go back down through the same stitch of R13/14. Make a knot on the inside of the head.

R17: (dec, sc in next 2 sts) 8 times {24 sts}

Begin to stuff the head and continue as you crochet. Make sure not to overstuff. You want the top and bottom to lay flat.

R18: (dec, sc) 8 times {16 sts}

R19: (dec) 8 times {8 sts}

Fasten off and leave a long piece of yarn to sew the head shut.

BIG CLAW

Make 2
Using color red
R1: 3 sc into a magic circle (3 sts)
Alternate way to begin: chain 2, sc 3
times in 2nd chain from hook {3 sts}

R2: (inc) 3 times {6 sts}
R3: sc in next 6 sts {6 sts}
R4: inc, sc in next 5 sts {7 st}
R5: inc in next 2 sts, sc in next 5 sts
{9 sts}
R6 sc in next 9 sts {9 sts}

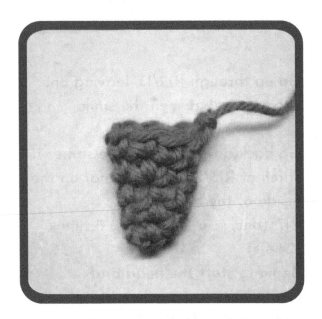

No stuffing needed yet. Fasten off
and set aside.

SMALL CLAW

Make 2
Using color red
R1: 3 sc into a magic circle {3 sts}
Alternate way to begin: chain 2, sc 3
times in 2nd chain from hook {3 sts}

R2: (inc) 3 times {6 sts}
R3: sc in next 6 sts {6 sts}
R4: inc, sc in next 5 sts {7 st}

R5: inc in next 2 sts, sc in next 5 sts {9 sts}
Instead of fastening off, grab the big claw and place it next to the small claw.

Single crochet directly into the big claw.
Go into the stitch next to the fasten off.

Continue to go around until you reach the end of the big claw.

Single crochet around the small claw until you reach the stitch marker.

Use the fastened off yarn to close holes between where the claws were joined, if needed.
The explanation above is considered R6.

R6: sc in next 18 sts around big claw and small claw {18 sts}
R7: (dec, sc in next st) 6 times {12 sts}
Stuff each claw but do not stuff anymore.
R8: (dec, sc in next 2 sts) 3 times {9 sts}

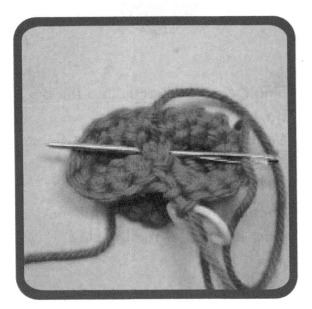

R9-13: sc in next 9 sts {9 sts}
Do a seamless join on an open piece:
Seamless Join Video

Cut the working yarn, leaving a tail. Pull the yarn through the last stitch (do not fasten off).

Thread the remaining yarn into an embroidery needle and insert the needle under both loops of the stitch to the left of the last stitch - from outside to inside.

Then insert your needle through the middle of the V - of the last crocheted stitch - from outside to inside.

Set aside until assembly.

MIDDLE LEG

Make 4
No stuffing needed.
Using color red
R1: 4 sc into a magic circle {4 sts}
TIP: Alternate way to begin: chain 2, sc 4 times in 2nd chain from hook {4 sts}

R2: (inc) 4 times {8 sts}
R3-4: sc in next 8 sts {8 sts}
R5: sc in next 2 sts, 2 dec, sc in next 2 sts {6 sts}
R6-9: sc in next 6 sts {6 sts}
Do a seamless join on an open piece as you did for the claw.

Set leg aside until assembly.
Note: The legs should have a bit of a curve from the R5 decrease.

For assembly, the curve should be on the bottom as pictured.

BACK LEG

Make 2
No stuffing needed.
Using color red
R1: 4 sc into a magic circle {4 sts}
Alternate way to begin: chain 2, sc 4
times in 2nd chain from hook {4 sts}

R2: (inc) 4 times {8 sts}
R3-4: sc in next 8 sts {8 sts}
R5: sc in next 2 sts, 2 dec, sc in next
2 sts {6 sts}
R6-11: sc in next 6 sts {6 sts}
Do a seamless join on an open piece
as you did for the claw.

Set leg aside until assembly.

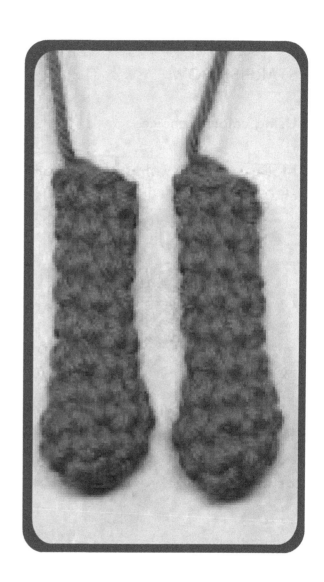

37

STARFISH BOW

Using color of choice

Make a slipknot with a long tail and chain 4

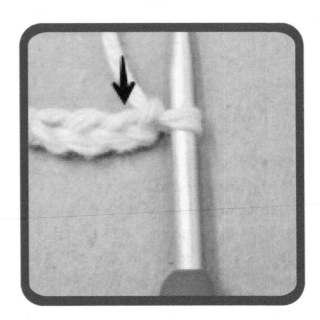

R1: sc in 2nd chain from hook, hdc in next st, sc in next st, sl st in same st as the sc {4 sts}

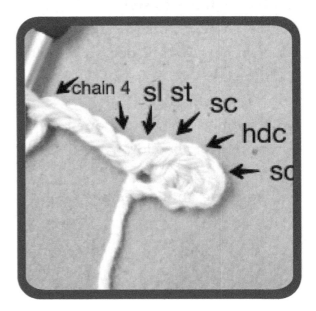

R2-5: chain 4, sc in 2nd chain from hook, hdc in next st, sc in next st, sl st into the hole next to the slipknot

Fasten off and leave a long tail. Tighten the yarn connected to your slipknot. Make a knot in the back to secure. Set bow aside until assembly.

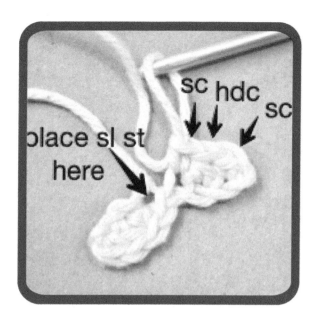

Attach the claw with the small claw facing up, between R12/13 and R15/16 of the head/body.

Leave one stitch open next to the embroidered eyes.
Attach the middle leg, one on each side, next to the claw between R12/13 and R15/16 of the head/body. The feet should have a bit of curve due to the decrease on R5.

Attach the second middle leg, one on each side, next to the first middle leg.

Attach the second middle leg, one on each side, next to the first middle leg.

Attach the back leg, one on each side, next to the middle leg between R12/13 and R15/16 of the head/body.

Attach bow between R7 and R8 by weaving the yarn through a stitch, making a knot, and weaving in any excess yarn.

Weave in all the excess pieces of yarn into the body.

Please be aware that amigurumi contains small pieces and can be dangerous to children. If you're selling this stuffed ami, please place a warning and also state that safety eyes are not recommended for anyone under the age of 3.

41

BENNY THE SEAL

MATERIALS

YARN: Light (3) in Light Gray, White, Light Brown; Classic Cotton Thread in Black

MATERIALS: C2 - 2.75 mm Hook; Poly Filling; Two 9 mm Black Plastic Safety Eyes

DIMENSION: H. 6" x W. 3.5"

ABBREVIATIONS: magic ring (mr), stitch (st), slip stitch (sl st), single crochet (sc),

back loop only (BLO), fasten off (F/O)

SKILL LEVEL: Beginner

INSTRUCTIONS: work in rounds

(join with a sl st and ch 1 at the end of each round) unless otherwise instructed.

MUZZLE (white yarn)

Rnd 1: 7 ch, 1 sc inc into the 2nd ch from the hook, 1 sc inc, 2 sc, 1 sc inc, 2 sc inc into the next ch, 4 sc, 1 sc inc into the last st that already contains 2 sc (18)

Rnd 2: 2 sc inc, 6 sc, 2 sc inc, 8 sc (22)

Rnd 3: working in BLO, sc even (22)

F/O and leave a long strand of white yarn to sew the muzzle to the body.

Embroider the NOSE with light brown yarn and a tapestry needle.

CAUDAL FINS (light gray yarn; make 2)

Make two:
Rnd 1: 6 sc in a mr (6)

Rnd 2: (2 sc, 1 sc inc) rep twice (8)

Rnd 3: (1 sc, 1 sc inc) rep around (12)

Rnd 4: (2 sc, 1 sc inc) rep around (16)

Round 5 - 6: sc even (16)

Rnd 7: (6 sc, 1 sc dec) rep around (14)

Rnd 8: (5 sc, 1 sc dec) rep around (12)

Rnd 9: (4 sc, 1 sc dec) rep around (10)

Rnd 10: sc dec around (5)

F/O and do not stuff the fin

Do not cut the yarn once you have completed the 2nd fin

BODY (light gray yarn)

Merge the two fins together:

Rnd 11: join the yarn with a sl st to the 1st fin you crocheted, ch 1 and sc in the same st, crochet around 4 sc, then keep working on the 2nd fin, 5 sc (10)

Rnd 12: (4 sc, 1 sc inc) rep twice (12)

Rnd 13: (2 sc, 1 sc inc) rep around (16)

Rnd 14: (3 sc, 1 sc inc) rep around (20)

Rnd 15: (4 sc, 1 sc inc) rep around (24)

Round 16 - 17: sc even (24)

Rnd 18: (5 sc, 1 sc inc) rep around (28)

Rnd 19: sc even (28)

Rnd 20: (6 sc, 1 sc inc) rep around (32)

Rnd 21: sc even (32)

Rnd 22: (7 sc, 1 sc inc) rep around (36)

Rnd 23: (5 sc, 1 sc inc) rep around (42)

Rnd 24: (6 sc, 1 sc inc) rep around (48)

Round 25 - 29: sc even (48)

Rnd 30: (11 sc, 1 sc inc) rep around (52)

Round 31 - 33: sc even (52)

Rnd 34: 28 sc, 8 sc inc, 16 sc (60)

Rnd 35: 28 sc, [(3 sc, 1 sc inc) rep 4 times], 16 sc (64)

Round 36 - 37: sc even (64)

Rnd 38: 28 sc, [(4 sc, 1 sc inc) rep 4 times], 16 sc (68); start stuffing

Round 39 - 41: sc even (68)

Rnd 42: 5 sc, 1 sc dec, 19 sc, 1 sc dec, 24 sc, 1 sc dec, 12 sc, 1 sc dec (64)

Round 43 - 44: sc even (64)

Rnd 45: 26 sc, [(4 sc, 1 sc dec) rep 4 times], 14 sc (60)

Rnd 46: sc even (60)

Rnd 47: (8 sc, 1 sc dec) rep 6 times (54)

Rnd 48: (7 sc, 1 sc dec) rep 6 times (48)

Rnd 49: (4 sc, 1 sc dec) rep around (40)

Rnd 50: (3 sc, 1 sc dec) rep around (32)

Rnd 51: (2 sc, 1 sc dec) rep around (24)

Rnd 52: (2 sc, 1 sc dec) rep around (18)

finish stuffing the body firmly

Rnd 53: (1 sc, 1 sc dec) rep around (12)

Rnd 54: sc dec around (6)

F/O and wave in end

Embroider the EYEBROWS and the EYELASHES with black cotton thread.

Embroider a contour around the nose and the line below it with black cotton thread.

PECTORAL FINS (light gray yarn; make 2)

Rnd 1: 6 sc in a mr (6)

Rnd 2: (2 sc, 1 sc inc) rep twice (8)

Rnd 3: (3 sc, 1 sc inc) rep twice (10)

Rnd 4: (4 sc, 1 sc inc) rep twice (12)

Rnd 5 - 6: sc even (12)

Rnd 7: (4 sc, 1 sc dec) rep around (10)

Rnd 8 - 9: sc even (10)

F/O and leave a long strand of yarn to sew the fin to the main body; do not stuff the fin.

Sew the right fin between rounds # 24-30, the left one between rounds # 39-44.

If you'd like to add more details to the seal:

· apply some blush to the cheeks using a little make-up brush,

· create the whiskers inserting little strands of nylon thread into the muzzle.

JUMBO PENGUIN

MATERIALS
Sweet Snuggles (jumbo)
(2 skeins) Pink
(<1 skein) White
(<1 skein) Yellow

NOTIONS
Size I 5.5mm Clover Amour hook
10.0mm safety eyes
fiberfill stuffing
tapestry needle
stitch markers

ABBREVIATIONS

ch: chain

CC: contrast color

dec: decrease

inc: increase (work two single
crochets in one stitch)

MC: main color

MR: magic ring

rnd: round

sc: single crochet

x sc: work x number of single
crochets

sl st: slip stitch

st(s): stitch(es)

(x sts): total number of stitches for
the round

(...) x: work all steps within
parentheses x number of times

TECHNICAL NOTES
Crochet in continuous spiral rounds,
unless specified otherwise. Use a
stitch marker or piece of yarn to
keep track of the last stitch in each
round.

Jumbo velvet yarn sheds very easily, so keep that in mind while working. When creating the magic ring at the beginning, pull the circle as tight as possible before working into it. Otherwise, sometimes the circle gets stuck and it's difficult to cinch tight.

If your amigurumi has gaps, size down your hook.

When filling with polyester stuffing, pull apart each large chunk into many smaller chunks. This ensures an even distribution of firmness within the amigurumi.

To make this amigurumi child safe, use black felt and hot glue for the eyes rather than safety eyes, which are not child-safe.

COLOR CODING
For this pattern, the MC is Pink, CC1 is Yellow, and CC2 is White.

FINAL SIZE
Approx. 10" (26 cm) wide, 12" (30 cm) tall

HEAD/BODY (in MC)

Begin: Chain 9.

Round 1: Beginning in the 2nd chain from hook, sc 7, 2 sc in the last chain, along the other side of the foundation chain sc7. For help on crocheting around a foundation chain, see here (16 sts)
Round 2: inc x16 (32 sts)?
Round 3: (3 sc, inc) x8 (40 sts)
Round 4: (4 sc, inc) x8 (48 sts)
Round 5: (5 sc, inc) x8 (56 sts)
Round 6: (6 sc, inc) x8 (64 sts)
Round 7-10 (4 rnds): sc around (64 sts)
Round 11: (7 sc, inc) x8 (72 sts)
Round 12-19 (8 rnds): sc around (72 sts)
Insert 10.0mm safety eyes between rounds 12-13, with 9 stitches in

between.

Round 20: (8 sc, inc) x8 (80 sts)

Round 21-24 (4 rnds): sc around (80 sts)

Round 25: (8 sc, dec) x8 (72 sts)

Round 26: (6 sc, dec) x9 (63 sts)

Round 27: (5 sc, dec) x9 (54 sts)

Round 28: (4 sc, dec) x9 (45 sts)

Round 29: (3 sc, dec) x9 (36 sts)

Stuff.

Round 30: (2 sc, dec) x9 (27 sts)

Round 31: (sc, dec) x9 (18 sts)

Round 32: dec x9 (9 sts)

Cut yarn, leaving a tail for sewing. Using a tapestry needle, thread the tail through the front loops of all 9 stitches in the last round, and then cinch tight. Bury the tail and cut the yarn (fig. 1).

WINGS (in MC)

Round 1: 6 sc in MR (6 sts)?
Round 2: (2 sc, inc) x2 (8 sts)?
Round 3: (3 sc, inc) x2 (10 sts)?
Round 4: (4 sc, inc) x2 (12 sts)?
Round 5: (5 sc, inc) x2 (14 sts)?
Round 6: (6 sc, inc) x2 (16 sts)?
Round 7: (7 sc, inc) x2 (18 sts)
Round 8: (8 sc, inc) x2 (20 sts)

Do not stuff. Flatten the wing so that your hook is on the right side, and then sc 10 through both sides of the wing. See fig. 2. Finish off, leaving a tail for sewing. Make another identically. Sew to the body between rounds 13 and 14 (counting from the top), 6 stitches to the left and right of the eyes.

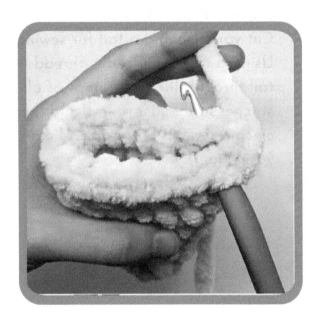

BEAK (in CC1)

Round 1: 6 sc in MR (6 sts)

Round 2: (2 sc, inc) x2 (8 sts)

Round 3: sc around (8 sts)

Round 4: sc around, slst to the first stitch (8 sts)

Stuff lightly. Invisible finish off, and weave in end, leaving a tail for sewing (fig. 3). Sew to the body between rounds 12 and 13. It should be directly between the eyes (fig. 3).

53

BELLY (in CC2)

Round 1: 8 sc in MR (8 sts)
Round 2: inc x8 (16 sts)
Round 3: (sc, inc) x8 (24 sts)
Round 4: (2 sc, inc) x8 (32 sts)
Round 5: (3 sc, inc) x8 (40 sts)
Round 6: 2 sc, (4 sc, inc) x7, 2 sc, inc (48 sts)
Round 7: (5 sc, inc) x8, sl st (56 sts)
Finish off, leaving a tail for sewing (fig. 4). Sew to the body between rounds 15-25 (counting from the top).

Your Jumbo Penguin is all done!

CECIL THE CLAM

hi ‑

MATERIALS
Crochet hook size: 5mm
  • #6 Super Bulky weight yarn: tan (outer shell), cream (inner shell), peach (clam), and 1 strand of pink (cheeks)
  • Yarn needle
  • One pair of 12 mm safety eyes
  • Polyester fiber fill stuffing
  • One strand of black embroidery floss for the mouth and eyebrows

Final measurement for the finished clam in his shell is 3.5 inches (or 9 cm) tall.

ABBREVIATIONS:
ch - chain
sc - single crochet
sts - stitches
dec - sc decrease st*

*Single crochet decrease stitch explanation:

Insert the hook into the next stitch and yarn over. Pull a loop through so that there are now 2 loops on the hook. Insert the hook into the next stitch and yarn over. Pull a loop through so that there are now 3 loops on the hook. Yarn over again and pull the loop of yarn through all 3 loops on the hook.

Outer Shell (x2)
With tan yarn,
R1: Ch 2, 8 sc in first ch (8 sts)
R2: 2 sc in each st around (16 sts)
R3: (Sc 1, 2 sc in next st), 8 times (24 sts)
R4: (Sc 3, 2 sc in next st), 6 times (30 sts)
R5: (Sc 4, 2 sc in next st), 6 times (36 sts)
R6: (Sc 17, 2 sc in next st), 2 times (38 sts)
R7: Sc 38 (38 sts)

Wait to fasten off until you have

made the inner shell pieces. Also, wait to crochet the 2nd outer shell until you have made both inner shell pieces.

Inner Shell (x2)
With cream yarn,
R1: Ch 2, 8 sc in first ch (8 sts)
R2: 2 sc in each st around (16 sts)
R3: (Sc 1, 2 sc in next st), 8 times (24 sts)
R4: (Sc 3, 2 sc in next st), 6 times (30 sts)
R5: (Sc 4, 2 sc in next st), 6 times (36 sts)
R6: (Sc 17, 2 sc in next st), 2 times (38 sts)

Fasten off, leaving a yarn tail for weaving in. You will now be crocheting the shell pieces together.

Insert your crochet hook back into the outer shell right where you left off at the end of R7. Then insert your hook through a stitch of the outer shell and a stitch of the inner shell, as pictured above. Single crochet all the way around the 2 shell pieces to join them. Fasten off, leaving a yarn tail for sewing.

Weave in the white yarn tail ends. Your shell will now look as pictured.

Now crochet the 2nd outer shell. As before, wait to fasten off and repeat the above steps to crochet the outer and inner shell pieces together (the only difference between the top and bottom shells is that you do not need to leave a yarn tail for sewing on the bottom shell, just for weaving in).

Using the 1 yarn tail you have saved, sew the 2 shell pieces together - when sewing them together, match up the 2 spots on the top and bottom shell where you fastened off so that seam will be hidden when you stitch them together.

With your yarn needle, make approximately 6-7 whip stitches to sew the top and bottom shell together, so that it opens as pictured below. Secure with a knot and weave in the end.

The Clam
With peach yarn,
R1: Ch 2, 8 sc in first ch (8 sts)
R2: 2 sc in each st around (16 sts)
R3: (Sc 7, 2 sc in next st), 2 times (18 sts)
R4: (Sc 5, 2 sc in next st), 3 times (21 sts)
R5-7: Sc 21 (21 sts x 3 rounds)
R8: (Sc 5, dec 1), 3 times (18 sts)
R9: (Sc 1, dec 1), 6 times (12 sts)

Pause here to put on the eyes and sew on the facial features.

Begin stuffing clam. Then insert the eyes between R7-8, with 4-5 sts in between. Firmly press the backs onto the eyes. Next, thread a long strand of black embroidery floss onto your yarn needle and insert it through the opening at the bottom of the clam and out between the eyes. Sew a horizontal stitch between the eyes on R7-8; then

bring your yarn needle up 1 round lower, grab the horizontal stitch and insert your needle back into the same exact spot, to create a "V" smile. Then weave the floss through the inside of the clam and out above the eyes. Sew 1 diagonal stitch above each eye for the eyebrows, as pictured below. Now weave the floss back through to the opening at the bottom of the clam, and tie the 2 ends of the floss in a knot. Tuck the ends inside the clam.

If you would like to add pink cheeks, thread a pink strand of yarn onto your yarn needle, insert it through the opening at the bottom of the clam and out right below the eyes. Sew 2-3 small sts to create each little pink "cheek" below the eyes (sewing just 1 stitch may disappear into the plush yarn; sewing 2-3 stitches on top of each other make the pink more visible).

Now go on to finish the clam:

R10: Dec 6 times (6 sts)

Fasten off, leaving a yarn tail for sewing. Finish stuffing the clam as needed - you want the clam to hold its shape but still be squishy.

Next, thread the yarn tail from the clam onto your yarn needle and weave it through the front loops of the remaining 6 sts from R10, as pictured below. Pull tight to close. Secure with a knot and weave in the end.

Place the clam inside his shell, and there you go, you are finished! Thanks so much for joining me in making this plush clam! Enjoy!

STARFISH

MATERIALS
(<1 skein) YarnArt Jeans (Sport)
Coral (Color #23)
(scrap) Wool and the Andes (Sport)
White

NOTIONS
Size D 3.25mm Clover Amour hook
4.0mm safety eyes
black embroidery thread
fiberfill stuffing
tapestry needle
stitch markers

ABBREVIATIONS
BLO: back loop only
ch: chain
CC: contrast color
dec: decrease
hdc: half double crochet
inc: increase (work two single
crochets in one stitch)
MC: main color
MR: magic ring
rnd: round

sc: single crochet
sk: skip
x sc: work x number of single
crochets
sl st: slip stitch
st(s): stitch(es)
(x sts): total number of stitches for
the round
(...) x: work all steps within
parentheses x number of times

TECHNICAL NOTES
Crochet in continuous spiral rounds,
unless specified otherwise. Use a
stitch marker or piece of yarn to
keep track of the last stitch in each
round.
When filling with polyester stuffing,
pull apart each large chunk into
many smaller chunks. This ensures
an even distribution of firmness
within the amigurumi.
To avoid large holes in the crochet
fabric, increase tension until the
holes cannot be seen, or choose a
crochet hook a size down.

63

Use sewing pins to secure parts of the amigurumi before you sew them.

COLOR CODING

For this pattern, the MC is Coral, and the CC is White.

FINAL SIZE

Approx. 2.5" x 2.5"

SIDE (in MC, make 2. See Abbreviations for meaning of "...")

Round 1: 5 sc in MR (5 sts)
Round 2: inc x5 (10 sts)
Round 3: (sc, inc) x5 (15 sts)
Round 4: (2 sc, inc) x5 (20 sts)
Round 5: (3 sc, inc) x5 (25 sts)
Round 6: (4 sc, inc) x5 (30 sts)
Round 7: (5 sc, inc) x5 (35 sts)
Round 8: (sc, *hdc, dc*, *dc, tr*, *2 tr*, *tr, dc*, *dc, hdc*, sc) x5 (5 points, 60 sts)
Invisible finish off, and weave in end. Continue to the face details

instructions, and then make another side identically, but do not finish off or add the face details.

The two nearest to the center for each line are small French knots, made by wrapping the yarn twice around the needle, and the last one is a larger one, made by wrapping the yarn four times around the needle.

The first knot is placed between rounds 3 and 4, the second between rounds 6 and 7, and the last knot on round 8. See Fig. 1 for placements.

Insert two 4.0mm safety eyes between rounds 5 and 6, about 4 stitches apart. Using three strands of black embroidery thread, embroider a "v" shaped mouth between rounds 6 and 7, right between the eyes.

Holding the two sides together with the right sides facing outwards, single crochet them together. Make sure that the side with no embroidery is facing towards you as you crochet the border.

Right before you finish crocheting the border, stuff the starfish with fiberfill. Slip stitch to the first stitch, invisible finish off, and weave in the end.

NO-SEW NARWHAL

MATERIALS

Hobbii Baby Snuggle (super bulky)
(<1 skein) Blue
(<1 skein) White

NOTIONS

Size F 3.75mm Clover Amour hook
6.0mm safety eyes
scissors
fiberfill stuffing
stitch markers

ABBREVIATIONS

BLO: back loop only
ch: chain
CC: contrast color
dec: decrease
hdc: half double crochet
inc: increase (work two single
crochets in one stitch)
MC: main color
MR: magic ring
rnd: round
RS: right side
sc: single crochet

sk: skip
x sc: work x number of single
crochets
sl st: slip stitch
st(s): stitch(es)
WS: wrong side
(x sts): total number of stitches for
the round
(...) x: work all steps within
parentheses x number of times

TECHNICAL NOTES

Crochet in continuous spiral rounds,
unless specified otherwise. Use a
stitch marker or piece of yarn to
keep track of the last stitch in each
round.

When filling with polyester stuffing,
pull apart each large chunk into
many smaller chunks. This ensures
an even distribution of firmness
within the amigurumi.

To avoid large holes in the crochet
fabric, increase tension until the
holes cannot be seen, or choose a

crochet hook a size down.
Try to avoid frogging velvet yarn since it sheds easily, and close the magic ring in the beginning as soon as possible, gently but firmly. Attempting to close it later on may result in breaking the yarn.
Use sewing pins to secure parts of the amigurumi before you sew them.

COLOR CODING
For this pattern, the MC is blue, and CC1 is white.

FINAL SIZE
4" x 4"

BODY (in MC)

Round 1: 8 sc in MR (8 sts)
Round 2: inc x8 (16 sts)
Round 3: (sc, inc) x8 (24 sts)
Round 4: (2 sc, inc) x8 (32 sts)
Round 5: (3 sc, inc) x8 (40 sts)
Round 6-7 (2 rnds): sc around (40 sts)
Round 8: (7 sc, inc) x5 (45 sts)
Round 9-12 (4 rnds): sc around (45 sts)
Round 13: (3 sc, dec) x2.
Create first flipper (tutorial here): chain 4 off the side of the narwhal, and beginning from the second chain from the hook, sc, 2 hdc, then work 1 hdc in the most recently worked st on rnd 13 to anchor the st (fig. 1 and 2). The flipper does not take up a whole stitch, and merely occupies the space between the last decrease and the beginning of the first single crochet in the next step. Continue working in the round: (3 sc, dec) x3.

Create the tail: chain 4 off the side of the narwhal, and beginning from the second chain from the hook, 3 sc back. Work 1 more sc in the most recently worked st to anchor. Then, chain 4 off the side, and sc 3 back,

69

work one more sc to anchor, then continue working on the round (See fig. 3 and 4).

Continue working in the round: (3 sc, dec) x3.

Create second flipper identically to the first one: chain 4 off the side of the narwhal, and beginning from the second chain from the hook, sc, 2 hdc, then work 1 hdc in the most recently worked st on rnd 13 to anchor the st (fig. 1 and 2).

Continue working in the round: 3 sc, dec. (36 sts total in round 13)

Insert 6.0mm safety eyes between rounds 12 and 13, 11 stitches apart.

Round 14: (2 sc, dec) x4, switch to CC1, (2 sc, dec) x5 (27 sts)

Round 15: (sc, dec) x9 (18 sts)

Stuff.

Round 16: dec x9 (9 sts)

Round 17: dec x4, sc (5 sts)

Finish off, leaving a tail. Bury the tail either by using a crochet hook or by using a tapestry needle.

70

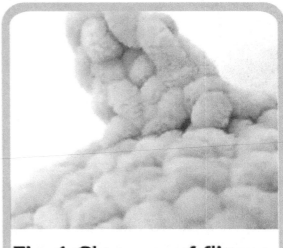

Fig. 1 Close up of flipper

Fig. 3: Close up of tail

HORN (in CC1)

Round 1: 4 sc in MR (4 sts)
Round 2: (sc, inc) x2 (6 sts)
Round 3: (2 sc, inc) x2 (8 sts)
Round 4: sc around (8 sts)
Gently stuff. Finish off,
leaving a tail. Using a crochet
hook, attach the horn to the
to the whale between rounds
3-5 (counting from the top),
directly between the eyes